30 day Prayer and Meditation Journal

to

Establish the

Kingdom Business

Mindset

(Thy Kingdom Come Series)

Christine Johnson

30 day Prayer & Meditation Journal to Establish the Kingdom Business Mindset

ISBN (978-0-578-78979-8)

Write Vision Publishing

Printed in the United States of America

Dedication

This book is dedicated to the amazing women in my life whom have had a tremendous impact on teaching me the power of pray, the results of prayer, purpose of prayer, pray without ceasing and prayer as an effective weapon. I am humbled, privileged, honored and humbled that God has given me to be birthed by you, taught by you and loved by you. Hallelujah!

The 30 day Prayer & Meditation is a remarkable tool to assist with pressing into the presence of God for revelation on how to implement God's effective plan and strategy with establishing the Kingdom Business Mindset. Establishing the Kingdom Business Mindset when embraced is the only way you can both understand your purpose, recognize God's provision, assess your performance, and grabbing hold to the truth which is your expected end is Victorious! Being about our Father's business is the only business we should care about. When we take care of His business, Our Heavenly Father will take care of our business.

Outline/Topics
Prayer (communication for direction
Purpose (call you out of darkness,
Platform (head and not the tale, prepare a table before
you, place you before kings, steps are ordered)
Pain (yoke is easy burden is light, suffering of this world
can't be compared, all things work together)
Provision (he will supply all your needs
Promotion (Kingdom and You) the LORD that promotes,
David as King, Esther, Ruth, Jesus,
Posture (Repent
Please God

Table of Contents

Let's Talk: Have you experienced any pain or discomfort in your walk with fulfilling God's plan for your life?

Let's Talk: What has our Heavenly Father spoken to you about your life and his plan? Is there any pain or hurt or questions you have about life and the direction of your life?

Let's Talk: Do you know about God's provisions for you here on Earth,? Your Role in the Kingdom's Agenda? Everlasting Life ? What provisions or resources do you believe you need?

Let's Talk: Have you postured yourself to receive from God? Explain your current posture (seeking God's direction, stewardship, sower, worshipper, obedient, willing, listening, etc.)

Let's Talk: Do you believe you are ready for promotion? Can you describe your character, integrity, work ethics, discipline, discipleship? Does this mirror the work and word of God?

Chapter 6 – Platform

Let's Talk: What has our Heavenly Father spoken to you about your life and his plan and ministry of Kingdom Economy? Do you know the platform God will use to implement the ministry He has called you to?

Chapter 7 – Prayer

Let's Talk: Have you committed and dedicated your life to a life of prayer? Do you have a prayer strategy? Are you passionate about prayer? Do you know the power of prayer?

Guidance in Scripture

Points to Ponder

Guidance in Scripture

Notes

Prayer of Salvation
& Confession of Faith

30 Day Prayer and Meditation Journey

God's Perfect Plan

Let's Talk:

*What has our Heavenly Father spoken to you
about your life and his plan?*

_____

_____

_____

_____

_____

_____

_____

_____

_____

_____

_____

_____

Pain of Purpose

Let's Talk:

Have you experienced any pain or discomfort in your walk with fulfilling God's plan for your life?

_____

_____

_____

_____

_____

_____

_____

_____

_____

_____

_____

_____

_____

Provision

Let's Talk:

Do you know about God's provisions for you here on Earth,? Your Role in the Kingdom's Agenda? Everlasting Life ? What provisions or resources do you believe you need?

_____

_____

_____

_____

_____

_____

_____

_____

_____

_____

_____

_____

Posture

Let's Talk:

Have you postured yourself to receive from God?
Explain your current posture (seeking God's direction,
In your stewardship, heart of repentance, as a sower, as a
tither, your giving, as a worshipper, your obedience,
willingness, teachability, etc.)

_____

_____

_____

_____

_____

_____

_____

_____

_____

_____

_____

_____

Promotion

Let's Talk:

Do you believe you are ready for promotion? Can you describe your character, integrity, work ethics, discipline, discipleship? Does this mirror the work and word of God?

_____

_____

_____

_____

_____

_____

_____

_____

_____

_____

_____

_____

_____

_____

_____

Platform

Let's Talk:

What has our Heavenly Father spoken to you about your life and his plan and ministry of Kingdom Economy? Do you know the platform God will use to implement the ministry He has called you to?

_____

_____

_____

_____

_____

_____

_____

_____

_____

_____

_____

_____

Prayer

Let's Talk:

Have you committed and dedicated your life to a life of prayer? Do you have a prayer strategy? Are you passionate about prayer? Do you know the power of prayer?

_____

_____

_____

_____

_____

_____

_____

_____

_____

_____

_____

Preface

Proverbs 2:2-6
King James Version

[2] So that thou incline thine ear unto wisdom, and apply thine heart to understanding;

[3] Yea, if thou criest after knowledge, and liftest up thy voice for understanding;

[4] If thou seekest her as silver, and searchest for her as for hid treasures;

[5] Then shalt thou understand the fear of the LORD, and find the knowledge of God.

[6] For the LORD giveth wisdom: out of his mouth cometh knowledge and understanding.

Introduction

But seek ye first the kingdom of God and His
righteousness and all things shall be added unto you.
To the only Wise and True God, Everlasting Father,
Maker of All Things, Alpha and Omega.
All honor and praise belong to you.
May this day continue to bubble with blessings and
overflow.
We know that all things work together for our good.
Beautiful are the works of your hand.
Merciful Mighty God All Power belongs to you.

Guidance in Scripture

King James Version (KJV)

1.) Matthew 6:5-15

2.) 1 Peter 5:7

3.) Hebrews 4:16

4.) Jeremiah 33:3

5.) Matthew 7:7-8

6.) John14:13-14

7.) Matthew 17:20

Please take the time, read and study the scripture.
Let's start the seek.
Amen.

Day 1

Scripture Meditation For the Week:

Our Heavenly Father, thank you for being God. We glorify you. We love you. Our intentions are to please you. Father be pleased with our worship and exaltation of your Holiness and Righteousness. Father you are merciful and greatly to be praised. Father have mercy on us. We repent of our sins In the name of Jesus. Any sin against thee by thought word or deed. Father thank you for forgiving us. We need you Father and our LORD and Savior Jesus Christ and the indwelling of the Holy Spirit. Father have your way in our lives. In you we breathe, move and have our being. We dare not try to do life without you. Father this day, is full of unexpected experiences, hidden things, mysteries revealed to the natural eye and mind. Father keep us secured in your arms, Keep your watchful eye upon us. Thank you Father. Reveal to us this day the provisions you have set assigned for the assignment that you have chosen for us this day. In the name of Jesus. Father and if we are not aware of what you have chosen for us this day, make it simple and plain for us to understand. Speak Father to your children in the name of Jesus. If fear, intimidation, discouragement, worry about the outcome try to settle in Father give us the courage, boldness, confidence, hope and peace to complete and achieve all that you have commanded us this day. In the name of Jesus. Father keep us in the name of Jesus. It's a joy to be kept and loved by you. Thank you Heavenly Father. God All Mighty you reign forever, you know all things, you see all things. So Father to stay at your feet for direction and instructions, leaning not to our own understanding but in all our ways we acknowledge you and you shall direct our paths. In the name of Jesus. Direct us. Father we turn our desires over to you in this day because we want to be in your perfect will for our lives. Your will, way and plan has surety, perfection, purpose and victory! We seek what you have ordained for our lives. Thank you Father. Our Father in Heaven we ask in the name of Jesus for your divine intervention upon our nation in the name of Jesus. We ask in the name of Jesus for peace and unity. We ask in the name of Jesus for your glory to rest upon this nation, community, city, state, government in every discipline, department and agency. Have mercy on us Father in the name of Jesus. Father allow you children to continue to be a light to our families, communities, city, state and nation. In the name of Jesus. Father have your way. We humble, surrendered, repented, obedient and yielded hearts this is

our prayer, supplication and petition before your throne of Grace. Heavenly Father and LORD Jesus Christ, Your Kingdom come Your will be done on Earth as it is in Heaven. We rejoice in you!

What tasks did you achieve today?

_____

_____

_____

_____

_____

What did you learn today about yourself, business, relationships, money, family, ministry, your gifts?

_____

_____

_____

_____

_____

Day 2

To God Be All The Glory. Father it is you that have made us and not we ourselves. The weight of your Glory bring us down to our knees. In your presence there's beauty and peace. According to your Word we have victory. ☐ Your Word is truth and life. You said man shall not live by bread alone but by every word that proceeds out of the mouth of God. Therefore we receive the truth of this day, and remain obedient to your Word. And all the blessings shall come upon us your children and overtake us because we obeyed the voice of the LORD our God. Blessed we are in the city. Blessed we are in the country. We're blessed coming in and blessed going out. Thank you for opening your good treasures of heaven upon us your children. Thank you for making us the head and not the tail. Thank you for making us above only and not beneath. Thank you for blessing the work of our hands. Our cups run over. Your love is indescribable. Merciful Father, All Mighty, All Powerful, All Seeing, All Knowing. God of All. With grateful humble repented hearts we glorify and worship you. Thank you for loving us and taking good care of us beyond what we can ask or think.

What tasks did you achieve today?

_____

_____

_____

_____

_____

_____

_____

What did you learn today about yourself, business, relationships, money, family, ministry, your gifts?

_____

_____

_____

_____

_____

_____

_____

Day 3

Great God, Most High, Strong Tower, Alpha and Omega, From Everlasting to Everlasting, Merciful, Faithful and True, the sea divider, mountain mover, healer, way maker, miracle worker. Your greatness is unsearchable, Your Kingdom is an everlasting Kingdom. With surrendered hearts we give you all glory. We bow down and reverence your presence. The weight of your Glory brings us to our knees. Be glorified. Be pleased with our worship Holy Father. Thank you for your precious thoughts you have towards us your children. Thank you for perfecting that which concerns us your children. Thank you for giving us your children Dominion over the works of Your hands. Thank you for this day full of blessings, ordained, assigned and appointed for Victory.

What tasks did you achieve today?

_____

_____

_____

_____

_____

_____

_____

What did you learn today about yourself, business, relationships, money, family, ministry, your gifts?

_____

_____

_____

_____

_____

_____

_____

_____

Day 4

All wise, merciful Father. The one and only true and faithful God. God Almighty. Us your children glorify and worship, we bow before you our Heavenly Father. Holy, Pure and Righteous are you. We approach your throne with humility. We repent of our sins any sins against thee by thought, word or deed. Only through your only begotten Son Jesus Christ are we able or this act of worship is even possible. Through his shed blood on Calvary for the remission of sins and present us faultless before you the only Holy God our Heavenly Father. Thank you Lord for justifying us. Lord Jesus thank you for your obedience even unto the cross. Thank you for leaving comfort to being wrapped in flesh to show us to way to a victorious life. Thank you LORD. You are the Lamb of God, Holy, Righteous King, LORD OF LORD, KINGS OF KINGS, our Savior, Redeemer, Healer, Teacher, Justifier, Our Banner, Standard, Guide, Friend, Comfort Giver, Living Water, Sustainer, Provider, True Vine, The Door, Great Shepherd, Wonderful Counselor, Our Rock, Our Strength, Our delight, the Light of the World, Rose of Sharon, Our Refuge, Our Hope, Strong Tower, Horn of Salvation, Lion of Judah, Our Love, Our Peace, Our Joy, Deliverer, Our Sanctuary, Our Victory. Thank you Lord for being more than we can every imagine. Thank you for being our overflow. Thank you for choosing us when we didn't even think of ourselves being worthy. Thank you for picking us up out of despair. Thank you for giving us a life designed to dominate and subdue the Earth and fulfill the Kingdom's mission. Lord thank you for salvation we rejoice in our inheritance. Thank you for never leaving us nor forsaking us. Thank you for reminders of who we are and whose we are. We are the redeemed, the chosen, the blessed, the loved, the provided for, more than conquerors in you, great we are in You because You are in us. Thank you for the favor of God active on our lives only because of You Lord Jehovah. Thank you for us being joint heirs because you have constantly made intercession and continue to make intercession on our behalf. Thank you King, Our Lord, Our Savior, thank you for delivering us the win. Thank you for giving an answer for us to the accuser of the brethren. Thank you keeping us and protecting thank you for being our LORD, nothing can compare. Thank you for giving us a name that is above every name. Jesus you are LORD and worthy to be praised. We bless your holy name. Your name is great above all the earth. Jesus we exalt you. We surrendered repented humble and obedient hearts to the service to our Father and King. We love you Father and Lord. Thank you for the indwelling of the Holy Spirit. This is our supplications, thanksgiving and prayer. Thank you for every blessing unveiled in this day. We rejoice.

What tasks did you achieve today?

_____

_____

_____

_____

_____

What did you learn today about yourself, business, relationships, money, family, ministry, your gifts?

_____

_____

_____

_____

_____

Day 5

Glory to the Most High God!! We exalt you and proclaim your Glory forever and ever and always. Heavenly Father so great is your mercy towards those who fear you. As far as the east is from the west. So far as He removed our transgressions from us. As a father pities his children, So the LORD pities those who fear Him. For He knows our frame. You guide, instruct and protect us. Thank for your love. Thank you your favour towards your children. Thank you for the open Heaven that hovers our your children. Thank you for our Goshen blessings that we live in. Thank you for the season of jubilee and overflowing. Thank you for sweatless victories. Hallelujah. Thank you when the enemy came in line a flood you have raised the standard! Thank you for the enemy fleeing in 7 ways. Arise O LORD and scatter all your childrens enemies. Nothing can stand against the armies of the Living God. Bring total destruction to every plan and plot of the enemy. Let every tongue that rise up against your children cleave unto the roof of the enemies mouth. Thank you for mighty angels of Heaven declaring war and victory on our behalf. Thank you for the sweatless victories. Hallelujah. We thank you and love you for being our God and Father. Although we know you have provided authority, power and dominion we come as your children humble and needy in your presence we can do nothing without you. With surrendered yielded and repented hearts In the name of Jesus this is our prayer and supplication.

What tasks did you achieve today?

_____

_____

_____

_____

_____

_____

What did you learn today about yourself, business, relationships, money, family, ministry, your gifts?

_____

_____

_____

_____

_____

_____

Day 6

Worthy and Adored You are Abba Father. God of All creation maker of Heaven and Earth. All power and authority belongs to you. Your children love on you, exalt you, worship you and give you praise. We thank you for your mercy, love, grace, kindness, holiness, righteousness, protection and truth. We yield and surrender all to you. We cast our cares upon you because you care for us. To your throne we submit our petition, prayer and supplications. You are the answer. Thank you for the battle that has already been won thank you for the victory you have delivered to your children. You are absolutely without question faithful, good, pure, honest. May our ears intentionally stay to your mouth. May our walk continue to be doers of your word. Our hearts love on you forever. Father take pleasure in our worship to you.

Love wins.

To every challenge you make us champion. To every difficulty you deliver us victory. To every problem you cause us to prosper. To Every trap you cause us to triumph. Thank you for keeping us secured with your watchful eye and mighty hand. Thank you that you are a Father that never sleeps nor slumber. Thank for designing us in your image to dominate. Allow us move and operate in full authority of the Kingdom of Heaven here on Earth. We humbly serve in full authority and capacity to fulfill your purpose in this life. Therefore we Walk and Speak with Love, Authority, Dominion, Precision and Power.

Day 7

But seek ye first the kingdom of God and His righteousness and all things shall be added unto you. To the only Wise and True God, Everlasting Father, Maker of All Things, Alpha and Omega. All honor and praise belong to you. May this day continue to bubble with blessings and overflow. We know that all things work together for our good. Beautiful are the works of your hand. Merciful Mighty God All Power belongs to you.

What tasks did you achieve today?

_____

_____

_____

_____

_____

_____

What did you learn today about yourself, business, relationships, money, family, ministry, your gifts?

_____

_____

_____

_____

_____

_____

Day 8

Scripture Meditation For the Week:

Ayyyyeeee. Yes. Worthy are you Father. All praises belong to you. Thank you for our LORD your precious Son Jesus, our Saviour and Redeemer. For you have formed our inward parts; you have covered us in our mothers womb. We will praise you, for we are fearfully and wonderfully made. Made in your image and likeness. Marvelous are your works ☐ Thank you for keeping us while we were yet disobedient, foolish, ignorant, distracted, deceived, unaware, impatient, judgmental, slow, making wrong decisions, in the wrong places and doing things our own wrong way.

You remained, never leaving us nor forsakened us. In the midst of our mess you kept us. Thank you for your unconditional love towards us. ♥☐

Thank you for your mercy and goodness. Thank you for hearing our cry, answering every call, wiping every tear. We give you all Honor and Glory. Thank you for every night of rest and everyday of peace. Thank you for a healed, restored, renewed, refreshed, revitalized life in you. Thank you for wrapping our lives with your mercy, truth and love. Father you are amazing, you are our answer.

What tasks did you achieve today?

_____

_____

_____

_____

_____

_____

What did you learn today about yourself, business, relationships, money, family, ministry, your gifts?

_____

_____

_____

_____

_____

_____

Day 9

Father you are absolutely amazing. Thank you for always showing up and showing out. Your WORD is true. You said you will do exceedingly abundantly above all we can ask or think. Thank you for being faithful to your children. Thank you Abba. There's no error in you. We lean not unto our own understanding but in all our ways we acknowledge you and you will direct our paths. LORD we thank you for being God with us, opening the door, showing us the way to life more abundantly. We bless the heavens this morning. May your Glory rest upon your children profusely and perpetually. Blessings overflowing our, cup runneth over. We receive in the Name of Jesus. We continue in this faith walk with declarations and decrees spoken and written by the Authority, Dominion and Power as joint heirs of the Kingdom. Father you are good. Hallelujah Blessings flowing. Seed growing, harvest blooming, Reaping coming. Hallelujah.

What tasks did you achieve today?

_____

_____

_____

_____

_____

What did you learn today about yourself, business, relationships, money, family, ministry, your gifts?

_____

_____

_____

_____

_____

Day 10

O Most High God, Our Father in Heaven. Early we seek your face, us Your children, the redeemed of the LORD. We delight ourselves in you and you inhabit our praises. We your children are blessed and rejoice because we put our trust in You. We shout for joy because You defend us. You are our reward, shield, strength, fortress, deliverer, safe place and refuge. Thank you for meeting us with the blessings of your goodness. There is no want to them that fear you. We shall not lack any good thing. Thank you for provisions in this day. This day is full of blessings and favour, protection, love, kindness, truth, wisdom, grace and mercy. We love you Father. With humble, surrendered hearts and a life yielded

to your will, plan and purpose we move forward
in full capacity with all authority, rights
and privileges of the Kingdom of Heaven.
For your good pleasure, Your Kingdom
here on Earth.

What tasks did you achieve today?

_____

_____

_____

_____

_____

_____

What did you learn today about yourself,
business, relationships, money, family,
ministry, your gifts?

_____

_____

_____

_____

_____

_____

Day 11

God of All, Heavenly Father, Sovereign God, maker of Heaven and Earth, Creator of All, Master, Your Majesty, All Knowing, All Powerful, All Seeing, All Wise, Alpha and Omega, From Everlasting to Everlasting. Father we glorify and magnify You. All your splendor cannot be compared. Father you are good and your mercies endureth forever. Father you are worthy to be praised. We give you all the glory. We worship you in spirit and truth. We bow down before you because you are God. Father thank you for this day that you have made. Thank you for the new mercies in this day that are so plenteous. Father we repent of our sins any sin against thee by thought, word or deed. Father cleanse and purge us, make us new. Bring us into right fellowship, relationship and oneness with you. Father our desires are to be pleasing in your sight. Father we can't do anything without you. Father, our desire is to be faithful in the things you have chosen for us to do in this season. Father speak in the name of Jesus. Heavenly Father we ask that your voice continue to be distinctive in our lives and we remain obedient to your will for our lives in the name of Jesus. Father we need you, the body of Christ need you, ministry need you, our spouses, our babies need you, our children need you, sons and daughters need you and family members need you, our military need you, our healthcare need you, our economy need you, our agriculture need you, our eco-system need you, our city, state, government, nation need you. Father in you we place our trust, faith and hope. There is no one else but you. Your grace, goodness, mercy, love, joy, peace and lovingkindness, righteousness and holiness.

Father look divinely upon us and allow your glory to fall heavily in the name of Jesus. Father we appeal your throne of grace with our petitions, prayers and supplications. You are God, We your children humbly and boldly according to your word, come to you. Father your word declares anything we ask in Jesus' name shall be given unto us. Father bring a love revival, Agape love, to be in love with you passionately, loving ourselves, neighbors, spouses, children, family, community, nation. Love heals, Love is patient, Love is Kind, Love covers a multitude of sin. In the name of Jesus destroy every plot and plan of the enemy that will breed hatred and envy. Father in the name of Jesus allow us to keep up our breastplates, shield, helmet, sword, feet shod, loins girded with your full armor. Bring your fire in the name of Jesus, Holy Ghost life transforming fire, In the name of Jesus. Fresh wind from the North, South, East and West. Blessings

overflowing. We receive in the name of Jesus.

What tasks did you achieve today?

_____

_____

_____

_____

_____

_____

What did you learn today about yourself, business, relationships, money, family, ministry, your gifts?

_____

_____

_____

_____

_____

_____

Day 12

Your word declares that we can ask you to hear us when we call, O God of our righteousness: You have enlarged and relieved us when we were in distress, have mercy upon us and hear our prayer. Father your word declares seek first your Kingdom and your Righteousness and all things will be added unto us. Merciful Father, All Mighty God, From Everlasting to Everlasting, Alpha and Omega, Beginning and Ending, Father you Reign Forever and Evermore. All Hail to the Throne of Mercy. God you are good and your mercies endureth forever. We place our trust in you. We place our love in you. Thank you for our LORD and Savior Jesus Christ your only begotten Son. It is He that have saved us and not we ourselves. Father have mercy. Thank you for covering us with your grace, mercy, love and goodness. Father we wholeheartedly repeat of our sins any sin against thee by thought, word or deed. Father continue to and guide us through this life of victory. We realize we are not longer captive or in bondage to sin, Father may the truth continually and forever be before us to deny ever lie, foolery, trick, falsehood and deception of the enemy that will try to lure us with our own lust, Father we deny every temptation in the name of Jesus. In you we are strong, we bring this flesh into captivity and thrive in the power and authority you have provided to us in the name of Jesus. Thank you Father for the Victory, in the name of Jesus. Arise, O LORD; O GOD, lift up thine hand: forget not the humble, in the name of Jesus. O LORD you are our strength, our rock, and our fortress and our deliverer, our buckler, the horn of our salvation, and our high tower, our refuge, our safety. Thank you. Father we trust you that our feet stand in an even place, victoriously, more than conquerors, with great works, life more abundantly. Thank you for the surety in you. Father in the name of Jesus direct us this day to every ordered step, every place you have prepared for us in the name of Jesus. Father we seek you first and your Kingdom, direct us in the name of Jesus. Thank you for the victory in this day. Thank you for the win. Thank you that every need is already met by through your will and hand. LORD thank you for covering everything you have assigned to my life in the name of Jesus. Thank you for keeping and watching over the purpose you have given each and every one of us, our mind, health, emotions, ministry, strength, family, spouses, children, parents, siblings, nieces, uncles, nephews, aunts, cousins, friends, home, business, inventions, finances, vision and destiny. Thank you for each area being promoted and prospering as you so declared. In the name of Jesus. Father we surrender all to you, we take our hands off of anything that you have not provided to each of us, each of us take hold with a passion that you have specifically given to us for the advancement of the Kingdom. Father and LORD Jesus we love you and adore you. With repented, obedient, surrendered, yield, humbled hearts to your will and way. Heavenly Father be pleased.

What tasks did you achieve today?

_____

_____

_____

_____

_____

_____

What did you learn today about yourself, business, relationships, money, family, ministry, your gifts?

_____

_____

_____

_____

_____

_____

Day 13

Merciful Father, Everlasting God, the Great I Am, A Jealous God, Alpha and Omega. With surrendered and repented hearts we give you all honor and Glory. We reverence you in spirit and in truth. Father thank you for Jesus Christ our Savior and Redeemer. Thank you for a detangled life. Thank you being a lamp unto our feet and a light unto our path. Thank you for a healed life. Thank you for a victorious life. Thank you for placing a watchmen at our minds, eyes, hearts, ears and tongue. Thank for a blessed life. Thank you for allowing us to be more than conquerors through Christ. Thank you for continuing to watch over us with your watchful eye. Continue to fill our lives with your love and strength. Your will, your desire for our lives shall continue to manifest bold and beautiful. Thank you for this life of purified trust in you, abundance, faith, love, goodness, kindness, tenderness, overflowing with blessings, wealth, good health, prosperity, happiness, joy, mercy, truth and grace.

_____

_____

_____

_____

_____

_____

What did you learn today about yourself, business, relationships, money, family, ministry, your gifts?

_____

_____

_____

_____

_____

_____

Day 14

To the all Wise, Merciful Father, Everlasting God, the Great I Am, A Jealous God, Alpha and Omega. With surrendered and repented hearts we give you all honor and Glory. We reverence you in spirit and in truth. Father thank you for Jesus Christ our Savior, Redeemer. We are more than conquerors through Christ. Thank you for a detangled life. Thank you being a lamp unto our feet and a light unto our path. Thank you for a healed and victorious life. Thank you for placing a watchmen at our minds, eyes, hearts, ears and tongue. Thank for a blessed life. Thank you for your watchful eye. Your will, your desire for our lives shall continue to manifest bold and beautiful. Thank you for this life of purified trust in you, abundance, faith, love, goodness, kindness, tenderness, overflowing with blessings, wealth, good health, prosperity, happiness, joy, mercy, truth and grace.

What tasks did you achieve today?

_____

_____

_____

_____

_____

_____

What did you learn today about yourself, business, relationships, money, family, ministry, your gifts?

_____

_____

_____

_____

_____

Day 15

Scripture Meditation For the Week:

Hallelujah is the highest praise Let everything that have breath praise the LORD. For He is good and worthy to be praised. LORD thank you for making every crooked path straight. That you for always being merciful and forgiving. Your love is impeccable. Your ways are flawless. Your WORD is powerful and sustaining. Your presence is marvelous and glorious. We yield and reverence all that you are. LORD we thank you for wisdom, peace, joy, family, friends, a happy home, servanthood, stewardship, seed, harvest, reaping, healing, love, nourishment, comfort, rest, vision, anointing, abundance, overflow, provisions, gifts, skill, talent,

Dominion, authority, power, diversified portfolio, sound mind, understanding, knowledge, creativity, selflessness, self esteem, humility, grace, goodness, mercy, truth, angels, guidance, hedge of protection, your blood, holiness, righteousness and salvation. Thank you for who you are and for who we are in you. Grateful to be loved by you.

What tasks did you achieve today?

_____

_____

_____

_____

_____

_____

What did you learn today about yourself, business, relationships, money, family, ministry, your gifts?

_____

_____

_____

_____

_____

_____

Day 16

Father where would we be without you? Where would we be without your precious Son Jesus Christ giving his life for us to have salvation? He stayed obedient unto the cross a merciless death he suffered for us, for us to have a choice, for mercy for us, for us to live a more abundant life, for us to have and truth, for us to know the truth and the freedom it provides, for us to experience the truth. Father our allegiance is to you and to your throne and our LORD and Saviour Jesus Christ. We need Jesus because in our best attempt in the flesh we will fail. Jesus is the completion. Jesus is the difference. Jesus is the perfection. Jesus is the strength of our life. Jesus be glorified. Father we love you, Jesus we love you. We honor and adore you. Father thank you for keeping us and allowing Jesus to continue to make intercession on our behalf. We know you and the power of your might as what you have revealed to us this day. Mysteries and Miracles. Father we pursue to keep experiencing you in a unique and soul satisfying way. Not just know of you like a subject but to experience you as Father and Jesus as LORD with all the greatness and goodness that you provide. Favour and Blessings. Love and Protect. Grace and Mercy. Father we need you all of you in every area of our lives. You are a good God and Father. Jesus you are LORD and great, We praise you and honor you. We repent. Father thank you for forgiving us of our sins in the name of Jesus. Father we seek your way and will for our lives continuing to be sensitive and obedient to your voice. You move we move. Father you are so amazing. We are awestruck. You are marvelous, exuberant, majestic, glorious, sweet, incredible, fascinating, stunning, stupefying, astonishing. Your faithfulness leaves us flabbergasted, astounded. Father we surrender, your way, your will, holiness and righteous call for our lives. Thank you for a perfected life through Christ Jesus. Thank you for allowing us to live under an open heaven. Father strengthen us on every leaning side for us to perform good stewardship of your provisions given to us. Father in the name of Jesus grant us wisdom to fulfil every assignment you have for us today. Thank you for the wealth that's revealed in this day. Financial blessings all throughout the day. Thank you for financial instruments expanding exponentially guide us how to use these tools to continue building your Kingdom here on Earth through making a positive impact for families and communities, for the unsaved. Let us continue to shine our light in darkness. Walking in love by giving to the poor and needy. May our behaviors and interactions today be pleasing in your sight. We surrender all. Thank you for the wealth that has been released materialized and manifested in the natural that cannot be quantified nor calculated by man. But every need supplied. May only you get the glory for this tremendous wealth movement on this Earth. May we stay humble. Thank you for the our cup running over. Thank you for the overflow. Thank you for every document that provides verification and attestation of the wealth that you have provided. May we continue to tithers, sowers, worshippers delighting ourselves in you and cheerful givers. May the wealth trail be seamless and endless. May the only explanation be the Will of God! Be Glorified! May every financial institution we come in contact with and choose be favorable and at peace with your children, in the Name of Jesus. Teach us and Train in the Holy Ghost! Wisdom we thank you for giving us the power to get wealth. Thank you for the Edenic Blessing, Abrahamic Blessing Thank you for being a covenant keeper to your children. We humble, surrendered, repented, obedient hearts to your perfect plan and will for our lives for the Kingdom being fully operational here on Earth. This is our prayer, supplication and petition. In the name of Jesus.

What tasks did you achieve today?

_____

_____

_____

_____

_____

What did you learn today about yourself, business, relationships, money, family, ministry, your gifts?

_____

_____

_____

_____

_____

Day 17

Wow. Wow. So good and true. Thank you Father for always being amazing and faithful. We bless your name. You are great, You do miracles great. Thank you for your astounding and abiding presence with us. There's no one like you. Father thank you for revealing yourself in a more intimate way. We desire intimacy with you. Father we repent of our sins and anything that will hinder a more intimate relationship with you. You make the difference in our lives. You have given us reason and purpose. We seek to be guided and directed by the power of your Spirit. Father we need you we can't do anything without you. Father In the name of Jesus we dare not to take a step without you. Father we walk by faith because of what you have promised, our confidence rest in you and not in the world. Father have your way in our lives. Father we surrender all to you. Have full access and reign in our lives. The extraordinary greatness that you have placed in us to exercise here in this Earth through gifts, abilities, talents and the power to obtain wealth. We humbly administer these blessings without regret nor apology. Father we stand with boldness and seek approval from no one for the spiritual gifting and authority that you have placed in us. With surrender humble hearts and yes to your will and way.

What tasks did you achieve today?

_____

_____

_____

_____

_____

_____

What did you learn today about yourself, business, relationships, money, family, ministry, your gifts?

_____

_____

_____

_____

_____

_____

Day 18

Our Father in Heaven, the lover of our souls, an irreversible love, a love that cannot be erased, hidden, overlooked, never forgotten nor mistaken. Father you are good and plenteous in mercy. You are kind and swift to our cry, your word says those that sow in tears shall reap in joy. You have caused our eyes to see Wondrous things from your law. Marvelous are all your works. So shall we your children meditate on them. Magnificent and Glorious is your presence. Your law is perfect. How sweet are your words to our taste, sweeter than honey to our mouths. Our lips shall continually utter praise. Our tongue shall speak of your word. Our hearts stand in awe of your word. As one who finds great treasure. We love your law.

We love you. Malak Yahweh. El Shaddai Thank you for prospering us, keeping peace and prosperity within our walls. We reverence you Father, loving on you forever. In Jesus Name, with repented, surrendered hearts we submit our prayer and supplication.

What tasks did you achieve today?

_____

_____

_____

_____

_____

What did you learn today about yourself, business, relationships, money, family, ministry, your gifts?

_____

_____

_____

_____

_____

Day 19

Father, we repent of our sins, any sins against thee by thought word or deed and any form of disobedience. Have Mercy on us in the name of Jesus. Thank you for forgiving. Your will, purpose and plan for our lives are perfect and flawless. Heavenly Father, Here is our worship, Receive our worship. You are Worthy. We have a desperation for your presence continue to descend and dwell in our worship to you. Your abiding presence is glorious and powerful. The weight of your Glory brings us to prostrate ourselves in worship. Our Master and King. We honor your presence. Hallelujah. Sweet Holy Spirit you are welcomed here, fill the atmosphere. Father we seek you intimately and passionately embracing your glorious presence. Speak to us. Speak guide and instruct. Speak Father we seek you as a child in need. We nestle in your presence and quiet ourselves before you the Living and True God. Speak. There's no other way, answer, wisdom, instruction, guidance, intellect, resolution, outcome, understanding or judgment besides what you have declared. We repent, yield, surrender and submit all and say Yes to your will and way.

What tasks did you achieve today?

_____

_____

_____

_____

_____

_____

What did you learn today about yourself, business, relationships, money, family, ministry, your gifts?

_____

_____

_____

_____

_____

_____

Day 20

He's worthy. Father with surrendered and yielded hearts to your will, we your children repent of our sins and any sins against thee, by thought word or deed. In the name of Jesus. Have mercy on us. Our Father in Heaven, great is thy faithfulness, morning by morning new mercies we see. All that is needed you have provided. There is no wisdom, nor understanding, nor counsel against the LORD. Jesus, the only name that's above every name and His shed blood that cleanses us of all unrighteousness. Deliver us. Restores us. Heals us. Strengthen us. Protects us. Sustains us. Thank you for being our strong tower, refuge, fortress, a hiding place. The only safe place, is in you. Thank you for your unfailing love towards us.

We love you we need you we can't do anything without you.

What tasks did you achieve today?

_____

_____

_____

_____

_____

_____

What did you learn today about yourself, business, relationships, money, family, ministry, your gifts?

_____

_____

_____

_____

_____

_____

Day 21

Heavenly Father with a heart of thanksgiving we thank you. Thank you for the Sun rising once again upon us your children. Thank you for our respiratory, skeletal, muscular, digestive, blood, cardiac vascular, spinal, brain, hearing, sight, taste, touch, speech are all working according to how you have designed, for our good and your pleasure, in the name of Jesus. Your will be done on Earth as it is in Heaven. This is the day that the LORD has made we will rejoice and be glad in it. Father with precision and exactness that can only come through your mighty hand annihilate, rebuke, destroy, eviscerate, make meaningless, insignificant, powerless, harmless, ineffective and impossible any attack or weapon formed

against your children in the name of Jesus.
Father we declare your presence power and
authority this day. We stagger not at what you
have promised to your children, children's
children and generations to
come. Thank you for loving us
with a vengeance. Touch not
your Anointed.

What tasks did you achieve today?

_____

_____

_____

_____

_____

_____

What did you learn today about yourself, business, relationships, money, family, ministry, your gifts?

_____

_____

_____

_____

_____

_____

Day 22

Scripture Meditation For the Week:

Without you where would we be, but God!! The earth is the LORD's and the fullness thereof; the world, and they that dwell therein. Father continue to teach us your children in the way that we shall choose. Our soul shall dwell at ease and you shall continually remind us of your covenant. According to your word you are our strength and the saving strength of your anointed. Father, continue to bless our inheritance, feed us with every word that proceed out of Your mouth, grant us peace and uphold us your children with your hand. Our inheritance is forever. You have ordered our steps and none of our steps shall slide. Father our trust is in you. Thank you Heavenly Father, we love you, we need you, we ask and receive from you, you have established your children here on Earth. Therefore we your children dominate, subdue, exercise authority, rejoice in you, receive power and strength by your spirit, healed, protected, delivered, shielded and set free, live in truth, walk by faith, prospering, living in the more abundant life and overflow. With surrendered humble hearts, thank you. Father.

What tasks did you achieve today?

_____

_____

_____

_____

_____

_____

What did you learn today about yourself, business, relationships, money, family, ministry, your gifts?

_____

_____

_____

_____

_____

_____

Day 23

Our Father in Heaven we praise you through song, dance and the instruments of clapping our hands, lifting our hands, moving our feet. Lifting all before you. Casting every care at your feet because you care for us. Father we bless you and rejoice in your goodness. You are so faithful, holy, righteous, good, magnificent, wonderful. Your love cannot be compared, questioned nor misunderstood. Father you are true to your WORD. Thank you for the Lamb of God. Bread of Life sent from Glory thank for giving us life, the abundant Life that can only come through you. Thank you for resurrection power. Father with are hearts in continual state of surrender we gladly avail ourselves to you. We repent of our sins and thank you for giving us your children. Thank you for the melody of love from you that is a sweet rhythm playing in our lives.

The song is written with well placed loops of grace, mercy in falsetto, the dun dun drum beat which declares your love for us and protection. We are happy to be chosen to hear and feel this awesome texture and touch of you. Father you are good. Our soul shall make a boast and be a delight in you. Thank you for your lovingkindness, sweet mercy, tender grace, goodness, provision. Thank you for the saving and healing name of Jesus, the only name above every name. No one greater, the Son of God, Jesus, Yeshua, Christ the Risen King, the Anointed One, Forever our passion and love. Here is our worship. Receive our worship.

What tasks did you achieve today?

_____

_____

_____

_____

_____

_____

What did you learn today about yourself, business, relationships, money, family, ministry, your gifts?

_____

_____

_____

_____

_____

_____

Day 24

To the Highest, our everlasting Stay, Almighty God, Merciful, Righteous, Upright, Faithful, Pure, whose way is perfect and girdeth us His children and has made our way perfect. Hallelujah. Our Father, Gracious and Holy we adore you, we love you, we thank you. In your presence there is fullness of joy. In your presence there is beauty. In your presence there is safety. Righteousness and Holiness dwells in your presence. Sanctity and Pureness in your presence. Father thank you for choosing us for your perfect will and pleasure. Thank you that you know every single hair, every move, every desire, every want, every concern. Father thank you for revealing yourself to us, your children, to have a powerful bond and relationship, providing to us wisdom, understanding, knowledge, our purpose. Thank you for your demonstration of love towards us through Jesus Christ your only begotten Son, Our LORD and Redeemer. Father have mercy upon us, in the name of Jesus. We receive your mercy and forgiveness. Father thank you. Father in this day is experiences we have never seen before. Father you are All Knowing, All Seeing, and All Powerful, Jesus is LORD of all according to your WORD greater works will we do. Father you have made us the head and not the tail, above and not beneath, a lender and not a borrower. According to your WORD everywhere our feet tread shall be ours, in the name of Jesus. Father according to your WORD, we believe by faith and have already received in the name of Jesus. We are more than conquerors, in you we live, move and have our being. Father we move in the authority that you have provided to us this day. Father our steps are already ordered by you. Father provide instruction in the name of Jesus. Thank you for the Victory. Thank you for the relationships being healed today. Thank you for mending broken hearts. Thank you for minds being stabilized today in the name of Jesus. Thank you for clarity in thought. Thank you for precision of speech. Thank you for the effectiveness of every step we take in the your name. Thank you for favour. In the name of Jesus. Thank you for preparing the way. Thank you for protection and covering in the name of Jesus. Father thank you for the Victory!! Hallelujah. Thank you for all things working together for our good. Thank you for the unbelieving that will believe in you and accept Jesus Christ as LORD and Saviour today. Thank you for the confession of Faith. Thank you for the backsliders receiving grace and mercy of repentance today. Thank you for revival and restoration. Thank you for the orphan receiving adoption today. Thank you for the healed today. Thank you for the recovered today. Thank you for hope being instilled today. Thank you for healing our land, in the name of Jesus. Thank you for never leaving us nor forsaking us. Thank you for maturity today in every area of our lives, character and investments. Thank you for doing the spectacular today. Thank for already having every provision in place. Father we ask in name of Jesus, nothing wavering that every utterance of prayer is answered we believe that we have already received in the name of Jesus. Father, we owe you the praise, Father you desire our praise, Father you are worthy of all praise and honor. Father we praise you lift you up and magnify you. We love you Everlasting Father, Almighty God. Father thank you for your thoughts for us are good, the plan you have for us are good, your way you have for us is perfect. Thank you

Sustainer, Faithful and True. With repented, surrendered, yielded, humbled, seeking, believing, faithful, unwavering hearts, Father do what only you the Almighty God can do. Hallelujah!! Hallelujah!! Hallelujah!!

What tasks did you achieve today?

_____

_____

_____

_____

_____

_____

What did you learn today about yourself, business, relationships, money, family, ministry, your gifts?

_____

_____

_____

_____

_____

_____

Day 25

Oh Yes it's a good thing to worship the Father in all of His splendor and majesty. Father it is you that have made us and not we ourselves. We lay at your throne in reverence of You Elohim Hayyim the only True and Living God. We love you. Father in the Name of Jesus we repent of our sins and seek your forgiveness and are forever grateful that only through your Son, our LORD, remission of sin is possible. Heavenly Father this world appears pleasurable, seducing the flesh to corruption in attempts to delay, distract and disrupt your perfect plan for our lives and the Kingdom's mission. So Father with a sincere heart mind and Spirit we go behind the veil.

We declare a reckoning against the enemies' agenda. In the name of Jesus. This season of your manifested Glory we receive with joy. Thank you for the supernatural, divine intervention and miracles. We bring this flesh under submission to the Spirit of God. We take confidence in the power of your WORD, believe and receive all the power and authority to transact sweatless Victories. Be pleased Father with our worship and obedience.

What tasks did you achieve today?

_____

_____

_____

_____

_____

_____

What did you learn today about yourself, business, relationships, money, family, ministry, your gifts?

_____

_____

_____

_____

_____

_____

Day 26

Father, we repent of our
sins, any sins against thee
by thought word or deed
and any form of
disobedience. Have Mercy
on us in the name of Jesus.
In the name of Jesus. Thank
you for forgiving. We don't want to be outside
of your will purpose and plan for our lives.
Heavenly Father, Here is our worship, Receive
our worship. You are the only one that is
worthy to receive everything we have. We have
a desperation for your presence continue to
descend and dwell in our worship to you. Your
abiding presence is glorious and powerful. The
weight of your Glory brings us to prostrate
ourselves in worship. Our Master and King. We
honor your presence. Hallelujah. Sweet Holy
Spirit you are welcomed here fill the

atmosphere. Father we seek you intimately and passionately embracing your glorious presence. Speak to us, guide and instruct. Father we seek you as a child in need. We nestle in your presence and quiet ourselves before you the Living and True God. Speak. There's no other way, counsel, answer, wisdom, instruction, guidance, intellect, resolution, outcome, understanding or judgment besides what the Almighty True and Living God has ordained and declared. We repent, yield, surrender and submit all and say Yes to your will and way.

What tasks did you achieve today?

_____

_____

_____

_____

_____

_____

What did you learn today about yourself, business, relationships, money, family, ministry, your gifts?

_____

_____

_____

_____

_____

_____

Day 27

Hallelujah is the highest Praise. Heavenly Father we honor you and bless the name of Jesus. We thank you for the Indwelling of the Holy Spirit. Father you know all things. Search our hearts, inner most parts of our mind and Spirit. Purge anything unlike you. In the name of Jesus. Father thank you for mercies renewed daily for us your children. Father we repent of our sins and ask for your forgiveness Thank you for forgiving us. Father you are worthy. And because of You we your children were born worthy. We are made in your image and likeness. Father thank you for the extraordinary gifts, greatness, power, provision, wealth, good health and abundance. Father we remain as children in your eyes. Thank you being attentive to our every move with your watchful eye. Take pleasure in us your children may we dominate and make an impact on this Earth. We move by your ordered steps. We reject any temptation to deviate us from your absolute perfect plan for our lives. We love you. We surrender. Always yes to your will Father.

What tasks did you achieve today?

_____

_____

_____

_____

_____

_____

What did you learn today about yourself, business, relationships, money, family, ministry, your gifts?

_____

_____

_____

_____

_____

_____

Day 28

Hallelujah! Our Father in Heaven, Our Great God! Thank you for your word, the only WORD of God. Thank you for the truth. Thank you for freedom and liberation in you. Hallelujah, thank you for freedom from bondage and captivity. We your children are no longer slaves to sin. Wherefore seeing we also are compassed about with so great a cloud of witnesses, let us lay aside every weight, and the sin which do so easily beset us, and let us run with patience the race that is set before us not anyone else's race, in the name of Jesus. Father we repent of our sins and any sins against thee by thought word or deed. Father have mercy upon your children this day. In the name of Jesus. Thank you for redemption.

Thank you for salvation. Thank you for life everlasting. Have mercy on us, Father in the name of Jesus. Have mercy on our nation, in the name of Jesus. Father we worship you in spirit and in truth. Thank you for being God. Hallelujah. Father thank you on this day and forever more for freedom to worship you, freedom to bring you glory and honor, freedom to give testimony of your goodness. Father we worship you God. Hallelujah. Father be pleased. Father thank you for your precious, righteous, holy, pure, loving, faithful and true and only Son, Jesus, KING OF KINGS AND LORD OF LORDS, Hallelujah. Father it's a privilege to be chosen by you. Hallelujah. Merciful, Magnificent, Excellent God. Worthy is the Godhead, Worthy is the Lamb, Worthy are you Father, Worthy is your presence of Holy Spirit, Worthy is your Word. Hallelujah Praise God Almighty. Father we bless you. Thank you for the gospel of Christ, for it is the power of you God unto salvation to every one that believe. According to your word and work Father therein is the righteousness of you revealed from faith to faith, we the just shall live by faith. Father we bless you our Creator. Thank you for giving us purpose, thank you for your perfect plan for our lives here on Earth. Thank you for the Kingdom Agenda that has already waged war and declared victory in the name of Jesus. Thank you for endurance to run this race that you have set before us. Thank you for the truth in you that we are more than conquerors in Christ Jesus. Thank you, Father. Thank you for every burden lifted, thank you for every care that we are able to lay at your feet, thank you for the increase and provisions to share in the name of the Kingdom of God. Thank you for meeting every need. Thank you for unity, peace, love, joy, gladness, happiness, renewing, refreshing today, in the name of Jesus. Father we come to you, we honor you, Father you are good and your mercies endureth forever, your grace is sufficient, your favor is unmatched, your word is incorruptible. Thank you for watching over us your children. Thank you for the truth, thank you for a solid and sure footing in you this day. Thank you for your glory upon us in this day. Hallelujah!! Your worthy, thank you for every answered prayer. Thank you for miracles, supernatural experiences, favor upon favor, faith upon faith, prosperity, wealth, abundance in this day. Father thank you for your watchful eye upon your children. Thank you for your hedge of protection upon us. Hallelujah. Thank you for the steps of Victory, thank you that our movement is ordained with your Authority in the Name of Jesus. Hallelujah!! Thank you for the anointing, power, authority and your decreed and declared word that we can speak for destiny to manifest in our lives, families, communities, nations. We go forward to do the work in the name of Jesus. Hallelujah. We give you glory Father and praise. With humble, repented, willing, obedient, surrendered hearts

hear our prayer in the name of Jesus, Father
may your will be done on Earth as it is in
Heaven.

What tasks did you achieve today?

_____

_____

_____

_____

_____

_____

What did you learn today about yourself, business,
relationships, money, family, ministry, your gifts?

_____

_____

_____

_____

_____

_____

Day 29

Glorious, Wonderful, Excellent, Majestic, Sovereign, Almighty God, Everlasting Father, The only true, the only God of All. Our Father in Heaven, God of mercy, Hallelujah, Righteous Father, Holy Father, we bow and worship this morning Father. Be pleased. Father we honor you, we adore you, we sing praises to you this morning, bless the heavens this morning, with bowed knees, hearts with full affection towards you. Our thoughts are overtaken by the blessings and love that you have shown us, the promises you have given us, your covenant you continue to keep, our LORD and Savior Jesus Christ your only begotten son, our door to you. Father we are humbled, we surrender all to you Father we pour our love upon you and your Son and Holy Spirit, Your Word, Your Truth, Father thank you. We love you. We are grateful to be called your children. Father bless you this morning. Father thank you for fellowshipping and communing with us this morning. May your presence settle here. Take up habitation dwell in our praise delight yourself according to your word. Father we are here at the altar of praise, glorifying you this morning. Father have your way. Father if there be anything that is hindering our praise Father remove it. Father we are here to bring you glory to be pleasing in your sight, have mercy. We repent of any sin against thee by thought word or deed. Father let not our praise or worship be hindered today. Purge us Father in the name of Jesus. Father we look to you in the name of Jesus. Only you can satisfy us in this life against the temptations of this world. Father have your way, in the name of Jesus. Thank you for this day that has beauty, pleasure, provision, joy, peace from on high. We receive the window of heaven pouring out today that we don't have room enough to receive. Father than you for being ever present, thank you for giving us what we need, thank you for loving us. Thank you for the truth that has set us free. Thank you for liberation. Thank you that you have revealed our true identity in you. Father Hallelujah thank you for choosing us. We are a chosen generation, a royal priesthood, the apple of your eye. Father thank you, thank you for the surety in you. Father Hallelujah, you are amazing (Heavenly Language). Thank you for every blessing. Thank you for delivering from dark and dangerous places. Thank you for shedding light on lies. Thank you for your truth about us your children. Hallelujah. We only receive your truth and identity. Thank you for intervening and disconnecting us from toxic networks and systems. Hallelujah. Thank you that the enemies plans were foiled, cancelled and rendered unable to be redeveloped. No weapon formed shall prosper. Thank you destruction upon the raging wolf that tried to disguise themselves in sheep clothing, thank you for the unmasking, thank you for the protection. Thank you Father in the name of Jesus. Thank you for the victory and the supernatural strength, thank you for the watchmen and and Heavenly Angels you have assigned to keep us in the name of Jesus. Thank you for every blessed step in this day. Thank you for teaching us your children obedience and how to yield to your command and instruction. Father in the name of Jesus, we submit our environment to you today. Provide the essentials and necessities for our environment to be fully functional according to your will and pleasure, stabilizing our environment bring natural balance sustained by the heavens. Hallelujah. Cleanse our environment only you can sanctify and sanitize. Father only you know all things. Cleanse our environment and bring an atmosphere whatever is in Heaven be loosed here on Earth. Father your Kingdom come your will be done on Earth as it is in Heaven. With willing, obedient, surrendered, repented, humble hearts, Father hear your children this day, be pleased, in the name of Jesus. We love you.

What tasks did you achieve today?

_____

_____

_____

_____

_____

_____

What did you learn today about yourself, business, relationships, money, family, ministry, your gifts?

_____

_____

_____

_____

_____

_____

Day 30

Scripture Meditation For the Week:

God of all creation, maker of heaven and earth. Master of all. Holy and Righteous. We bow, we worship, we adore you, we love you, we surrender all. Our Sovereign God. Eminent, immutable, all power belongs to you. We bow, we worship, we praise you in song, dance, clapping our hands, in obedience. You are God and merciful, Just and pure. Father there is no like you. You have given us triumph to triumph and brought us victory through Jesus Christ your only begotten Son. Thank you for salvation and life everlasting. Father thank you for being so gracious and kind to our LORD Jesus. Father you have kept every word and promise to our KIng. Father you said He will reign with you and indeed He is. Thank you that because of your righteousness and truth we all live a life of victory, authority, grace, love, holiness, power and unity. Thank you Father we love you. Thank you Jesus for continuing to make intercession on our behalf and the Holy Spirit continues to comfort us and guide us. Hallelujah!! We are free. No more bondage, no more captivity. Saved by the mighty hand of our All Mighty God and Father. Hallelujah. We repent of any sin against thee by thought word or deed. Thank Father for forgiving us and new mercies received daily thank you for the provision of mercy. Hallelujah thank you for the reconciliation and redemption. Hallelujah!!! You reign forever and ever more. All Hail King Jesus who causes us to triumph. Hallelujah. Father in the name of

Jesus we cast every care at your feet today. Anyone that may have a worry or feelings of being overwhelmed, fearful, discouraged, isolated, paranoid, hopeless, confused, lost, rejected, abandoned, victimized, hurt, the sick, disappointed, left out, stigmatized, ridiculed, hungry, homeless, worthless, penniless, broke, poverty stricken, dumb, stupid, unnecessary, purposeless, useless. Father in the Name of Jesus bring your Spirit, Your Presence, Your Touch, Your Voice, Your Anointing, Your Grace, Your Mercy, Your Word, Your Truth, Your Your Vision, Your Love, Your Hope, Your Angels, Your Wisdom, Your Faith, Your instruction, Your Comfort, Your truth, Your way, Your perfect plan, save, deliver, set free, change lives today in the name of Jesus. Hallelujah, destroy the wicked plan of the enemy in this hour. We declare victory today for the unsaved, lost, backsliders, sisters and brothers. In the name of Jesus, Father in the name of Jesus let us continue to do the work of the Kingdom, serving, giving, walking in love, unity, happiness, peace. In the name of Jesus. O God our Helper, have your way today. Settle here, bring love, faith, joy, peace and restoration, unity, revival, hope, goodness, kindness, humility, soundness, righteousness, holiness, provision and resources, financial breakthroughs, overflow and abundance, wealth transference, revelation, vision. Father all sufficiency is in you. Thank you for healing your people and healing our land. You are worthy to be praised. Father we yield, are hearts are surrendered, our hands are open wide to serve, ready to give, our hearts are open to love, our arms ready to comfort, our shoulders ready to support, our feet in obedience to the steps you have ordered, our tongue stay in obedience to your instruction our voice are lifted as you have tempered them, our minds stay on you and the mission of the Kingdom, we deny ourselves today in the name of Jesus. With repented, surrendered, yielded and wiling and obedient hearts. Hear our, your children, prayer, petition, supplication we ask in the name of Jesus.

Points to Ponder

- Put God First and Make your Relationship with Him a priority
- Dedicate time to prayer
- Practice the Presence of God
- Get your Vision Board Up Close and Personal
- Stay Focused
- Meditate on God's Word Daily
- Pray without ceasing
- Don't waste Time, Money, Energy
- Practice Good Stewardship
- Continue Tithing
- Continuing Giving
- Continue Worshipping our Almighty God
- Open Ways for God to Bless you and send provisions such as bank accounts, relationships, ideas Has given to you, gifts He has given to you, skills and talents He has given to you, Abilities He has given to you. All for His Glory and Purpose.

Guidance in Scripture

King James Version (KJV)

1.) Ephesians 3:20

2.) Psalm 37:4-5

3.) Luke 6:38

4.) Mark 11:24

5.) Hebrews 11:6

6.) Proverbs 3:5-6

7.) Philippians 4:19

8.) Psalm 138:8

Please take the time, read and study the scripture.
Our Heavenly Father watches over His Word.
Amen.

Notes

_____

_____

_____

_____

_____

_____

_____

_____

_____

_____

_____

_____

_____

Notes

Prayer of Salvation

Romans 10:13-17: For whosoever shall call upon the name of the Lord shall be saved. [14] How then shall they call on him in whom they have not believed? and how shall they believe in him of whom they have not heard? and how shall they hear without a preacher? [15] and how shall they preach, except they be sent? as it is written, How beautiful are the feet of them that preach the gospel of peace, and bring glad tidings of good things! [16] But they have not all obeyed the gospel. For Esaias (Isaiah) saith, Lord, who hath believed our report? [17] So then faith *cometh* by hearing, and hearing by the word of God.

Personal Confession of Faith

O Lord, I know I'm a sinner. I believe Jesus Christ died for me. And I believe with all my heart that He arose from the dead. I ask you to save me right now and give me everlasting life. I believe in Jesus Christ, and I trust you to save me.
Amen!

Hallelujah!!   Hallelujah!!   Hallelujah!!

To Contact the Author:

Write Vision Publishing, LLC
PO Box 25845
Richmond, Virginia 23260
admin@writevisionpublishing.com

30 day Prayer and Meditation Journal
to
Establish the
Kingdom Business Mindset

(Thy Kingdom Come Series)

Write Vision Publishing, LLC | PO Box 25845 | Richmond, Virginia 23260

www.ingramcontent.com/pod-product-compliance
Lightning Source LLC
Chambersburg PA
CBHW021940190326
41519CB00009B/1079